AUTO MILEAGE LOG

Copyright 2014

MILEAGE LOG

DATE	BUSINESS PURPOSE			
DATE				

MILEAGE LOG

METER READING		BUSINESS MILES	COMMUTER MILES	PERSONAL MILES
BEGIN	END			

MILEAGE LOG

DATE	BUSINESS PURPOSE			
DATE	BUSINESS PURPOSE			

MILEAGE LOG

| METER READING | | BUSINESS MILES | COMMUTER MILES | PERSONAL MILES |
BEGIN	END			

MILEAGE LOG

DATE	BUSINESS PURPOSE			
DATE	BUSINESS PURPOSE			

MILEAGE LOG

METER READING		BUSINESS MILES	COMMUTER MILES	PERSONAL MILES
BEGIN	END			

MILEAGE LOG

DATE		BUSINESS PURPOSE		
DATE		BUSINESS PURPOSE		

MILEAGE LOG

METER READING		BUSINESS MILES	COMMUTER MILES	PERSONAL MILES
BEGIN	END			

MILEAGE LOG

DATE	BUSINESS PURPOSE			
DATE	BUSINESS PURPOSE			

MILEAGE LOG

METER READING		BUSINESS MILES	COMMUTER MILES	PERSONAL MILES
BEGIN	END			

MILEAGE LOG

DATE	BUSINESS PURPOSE			
DATE	BUSINESS PURPOSE			

MILEAGE LOG

METER READING		BUSINESS MILES	COMMUTER MILES	PERSONAL MILES
BEGIN	END			

MILEAGE LOG

DATE	BUSINESS PURPOSE			

MILEAGE LOG

METER READING		BUSINESS MILES	COMMUTER MILES	PERSONAL MILES
BEGIN	END			

MILEAGE LOG

DATE	BUSINESS PURPOSE			
DATE	BUSINESS PURPOSE			

MILEAGE LOG

METER READING		BUSINESS MILES	COMMUTER MILES	PERSONAL MILES
BEGIN	END			

MILEAGE LOG

DATE	BUSINESS PURPOSE			
DATE	BUSINESS PURPOSE			

MILEAGE LOG

METER READING		BUSINESS MILES	COMMUTER MILES	PERSONAL MILES
BEGIN	END			

MILEAGE LOG

DATE	BUSINESS PURPOSE			
DATE	BUSINESS PURPOSE			

MILEAGE LOG

METER READING		BUSINESS MILES	COMMUTER MILES	PERSONAL MILES
BEGIN	END			

MILEAGE LOG

DATE	BUSINESS PURPOSE			

MILEAGE LOG

| METER READING | | BUSINESS MILES | COMMUTER MILES | PERSONAL MILES |
BEGIN	END			

MILEAGE LOG

DATE	BUSINESS PURPOSE			

MILEAGE LOG

METER READING		BUSINESS MILES	COMMUTER MILES	PERSONAL MILES
BEGIN	END			

MILEAGE LOG

DATE	BUSINESS PURPOSE			
DATE	BUSINESS PURPOSE			

MILEAGE LOG

METER READING		BUSINESS MILES	COMMUTER MILES	PERSONAL MILES
BEGIN	END			

MILEAGE LOG

DATE	BUSINESS PURPOSE			

MILEAGE LOG

METER READING		BUSINESS MILES	COMMUTER MILES	PERSONAL MILES
BEGIN	END			

MILEAGE LOG

DATE		BUSINESS PURPOSE		

MILEAGE LOG

METER READING		BUSINESS MILES	COMMUTER MILES	PERSONAL MILES
BEGIN	END			

MILEAGE LOG

DATE	BUSINESS PURPOSE			
DATE	BUSINESS PURPOSE			

MILEAGE LOG

METER READING		BUSINESS MILES	COMMUTER MILES	PERSONAL MILES
BEGIN	END			

MILEAGE LOG

DATE	BUSINESS PURPOSE			
DATE	BUSINESS PURPOSE			

MILEAGE LOG

METER READING		BUSINESS MILES	COMMUTER MILES	PERSONAL MILES
BEGIN	END			

MILEAGE LOG

DATE	BUSINESS PURPOSE			

MILEAGE LOG

| METER READING | | BUSINESS MILES | COMMUTER MILES | PERSONAL MILES |
BEGIN	END			

MILEAGE LOG

DATE	BUSINESS PURPOSE			
DATE	BUSINESS PURPOSE			

MILEAGE LOG

METER READING		BUSINESS MILES	COMMUTER MILES	PERSONAL MILES
BEGIN	END			

MILEAGE LOG

DATE		BUSINESS PURPOSE		
DATE		BUSINESS PURPOSE		

MILEAGE LOG

METER READING		BUSINESS MILES	COMMUTER MILES	PERSONAL MILES
BEGIN	END			

MILEAGE LOG

DATE	BUSINESS PURPOSE			

MILEAGE LOG

METER READING		BUSINESS MILES	COMMUTER MILES	PERSONAL MILES
BEGIN	END			
BEGIN	END	BUSINESS MILES	COMMUTER MILES	PERSONAL MILES

MILEAGE LOG

DATE		BUSINESS PURPOSE		
DATE		BUSINESS PURPOSE		

MILEAGE LOG

METER READING		BUSINESS MILES	COMMUTER MILES	PERSONAL MILES
BEGIN	END			

MILEAGE LOG

DATE	BUSINESS PURPOSE			
DATE	BUSINESS PURPOSE			

MILEAGE LOG

METER READING		BUSINESS MILES	COMMUTER MILES	PERSONAL MILES
BEGIN	END			

MILEAGE LOG

DATE	BUSINESS PURPOSE			
DATE	BUSINESS PURPOSE			

MILEAGE LOG

METER READING		BUSINESS MILES	COMMUTER MILES	PERSONAL MILES
BEGIN	END			

MILEAGE LOG

DATE	BUSINESS PURPOSE			

MILEAGE LOG

| METER READING | | BUSINESS MILES | COMMUTER MILES | PERSONAL MILES |
BEGIN	END			

MILEAGE LOG

DATE	BUSINESS PURPOSE			
DATE	BUSINESS PURPOSE			

MILEAGE LOG

METER READING		BUSINESS MILES	COMMUTER MILES	PERSONAL MILES
BEGIN	END			

MILEAGE LOG

DATE	BUSINESS PURPOSE			

MILEAGE LOG

METER READING		BUSINESS MILES	COMMUTER MILES	PERSONAL MILES
BEGIN	END			

MILEAGE LOG

DATE	BUSINESS PURPOSE			
DATE	BUSINESS PURPOSE			

MILEAGE LOG

METER READING		BUSINESS MILES	COMMUTER MILES	PERSONAL MILES
BEGIN	END			

MILEAGE LOG

DATE	BUSINESS PURPOSE			
DATE	BUSINESS PURPOSE			

MILEAGE LOG

METER READING		BUSINESS MILES	COMMUTER MILES	PERSONAL MILES
BEGIN	END			

MILEAGE LOG

DATE	BUSINESS PURPOSE			

MILEAGE LOG

METER READING		BUSINESS MILES	COMMUTER MILES	PERSONAL MILES
BEGIN	END			

MILEAGE LOG

DATE	BUSINESS PURPOSE			
DATE	BUSINESS PURPOSE			

MILEAGE LOG

METER READING		BUSINESS MILES	COMMUTER MILES	PERSONAL MILES
BEGIN	END			
BEGIN	END	BUSINESS MILES	COMMUTER MILES	PERSONAL MILES

MILEAGE LOG

DATE	BUSINESS PURPOSE			

MILEAGE LOG

METER READING		BUSINESS MILES	COMMUTER MILES	PERSONAL MILES
BEGIN	END			

MILEAGE LOG

DATE	BUSINESS PURPOSE			
DATE	BUSINESS PURPOSE			

MILEAGE LOG

METER READING		BUSINESS MILES	COMMUTER MILES	PERSONAL MILES
BEGIN	END			
BEGIN	END	BUSINESS MILES	COMMUTER MILES	PERSONAL MILES

MILEAGE LOG

DATE	BUSINESS PURPOSE			
DATE				

MILEAGE LOG

METER READING		BUSINESS MILES	COMMUTER MILES	PERSONAL MILES
BEGIN	END			

MILEAGE LOG

DATE	BUSINESS PURPOSE			

MILEAGE LOG

METER READING		BUSINESS MILES	COMMUTER MILES	PERSONAL MILES
BEGIN	END			

MILEAGE LOG

DATE	BUSINESS PURPOSE			
DATE	BUSINESS PURPOSE			

MILEAGE LOG

METER READING		BUSINESS MILES	COMMUTER MILES	PERSONAL MILES
BEGIN	END			

MILEAGE LOG

DATE	BUSINESS PURPOSE			
DATE				

MILEAGE LOG

METER READING		BUSINESS MILES	COMMUTER MILES	PERSONAL MILES
BEGIN	END			

MILEAGE LOG

DATE	BUSINESS PURPOSE			
DATE	BUSINESS PURPOSE			

MILEAGE LOG

METER READING		BUSINESS MILES	COMMUTER MILES	PERSONAL MILES
BEGIN	END			

MILEAGE LOG

DATE		BUSINESS PURPOSE		
DATE		BUSINESS PURPOSE		

MILEAGE LOG

| METER READING | | BUSINESS MILES | COMMUTER MILES | PERSONAL MILES |
BEGIN	END			

MILEAGE LOG

DATE	BUSINESS PURPOSE			
DATE	BUSINESS PURPOSE			

MILEAGE LOG

METER READING		BUSINESS MILES	COMMUTER MILES	PERSONAL MILES
BEGIN	END			

MILEAGE LOG

DATE	BUSINESS PURPOSE			
DATE				

MILEAGE LOG

METER READING		BUSINESS MILES	COMMUTER MILES	PERSONAL MILES
BEGIN	END			

MILEAGE LOG

DATE		BUSINESS PURPOSE		
DATE		BUSINESS PURPOSE		

MILEAGE LOG

METER READING		BUSINESS MILES	COMMUTER MILES	PERSONAL MILES
BEGIN	END			

MILEAGE LOG

DATE	BUSINESS PURPOSE			
DATE	BUSINESS PURPOSE			

MILEAGE LOG

METER READING		BUSINESS MILES	COMMUTER MILES	PERSONAL MILES
BEGIN	END			
BEGIN	END			

MILEAGE LOG

DATE	BUSINESS PURPOSE			

MILEAGE LOG

| METER READING | | BUSINESS MILES | COMMUTER MILES | PERSONAL MILES |
BEGIN	END			

MILEAGE LOG

DATE	BUSINESS PURPOSE			
DATE	BUSINESS PURPOSE			

MILEAGE LOG

METER READING		BUSINESS MILES	COMMUTER MILES	PERSONAL MILES
BEGIN	END			

MILEAGE LOG

DATE	BUSINESS PURPOSE			
DATE				

MILEAGE LOG

METER READING		BUSINESS MILES	COMMUTER MILES	PERSONAL MILES
BEGIN	END			

MILEAGE LOG

DATE	BUSINESS PURPOSE			

MILEAGE LOG

METER READING		BUSINESS MILES	COMMUTER MILES	PERSONAL MILES
BEGIN	END			
BEGIN	END	BUSINESS MILES	COMMUTER MILES	PERSONAL MILES

MILEAGE LOG

DATE	BUSINESS PURPOSE			
DATE				

MILEAGE LOG

METER READING		BUSINESS MILES	COMMUTER MILES	PERSONAL MILES
BEGIN	END			

MILEAGE LOG

DATE	BUSINESS PURPOSE			
DATE	BUSINESS PURPOSE			

MILEAGE LOG

METER READING		BUSINESS MILES	COMMUTER MILES	PERSONAL MILES
BEGIN	END			